FAR BEYOND
THE
GARDEN GATE

Alexandra David-Neel's Journey to Lhasa

Don Brown

Houghton Mifflin Company Boston 2002

For Ellen and Steve, with love

The text of this book is set in Hiroshige.
The illustrations are pen and ink and watercolor on paper.
Calligraphy by Deborah Nadel

Library of Congress Cataloging-in-Publication Data

Brown, Don.
Far beyond the garden gate : Alexandra David-Neel's journey to Lhasa / by Don Brown.
p. cm.
Includes bibliographical references.
Summary: Describes the life and travels of Alexandra David-Neel, who became a
scholar of Buddhism and Tibet in the early twentieth century and trekked thousands
of miles to reach Lhasa, the Tibetan capital.
ISBN 0-618-08364-2 (hardcover)
1. David-Neel, Alexandra, 1868–1969—Journeys—China—Lhasa—Juvenile literature.
2. Lhasa (China)—Description and travel—Juvenile literature. [1. David-Neel,
Alexandra, 1868–1969. 2. Travelers. 3. Buddhists. 4. Tibet (China)—Description and
travel. 5. Voyages and travels.] I. Title.
DS797.82.L45 D384 2002
915.1'5—dc21
2002000222

Manufactured in the United States of America
PHX 10 9 8 7 6 5 4 3 2 1

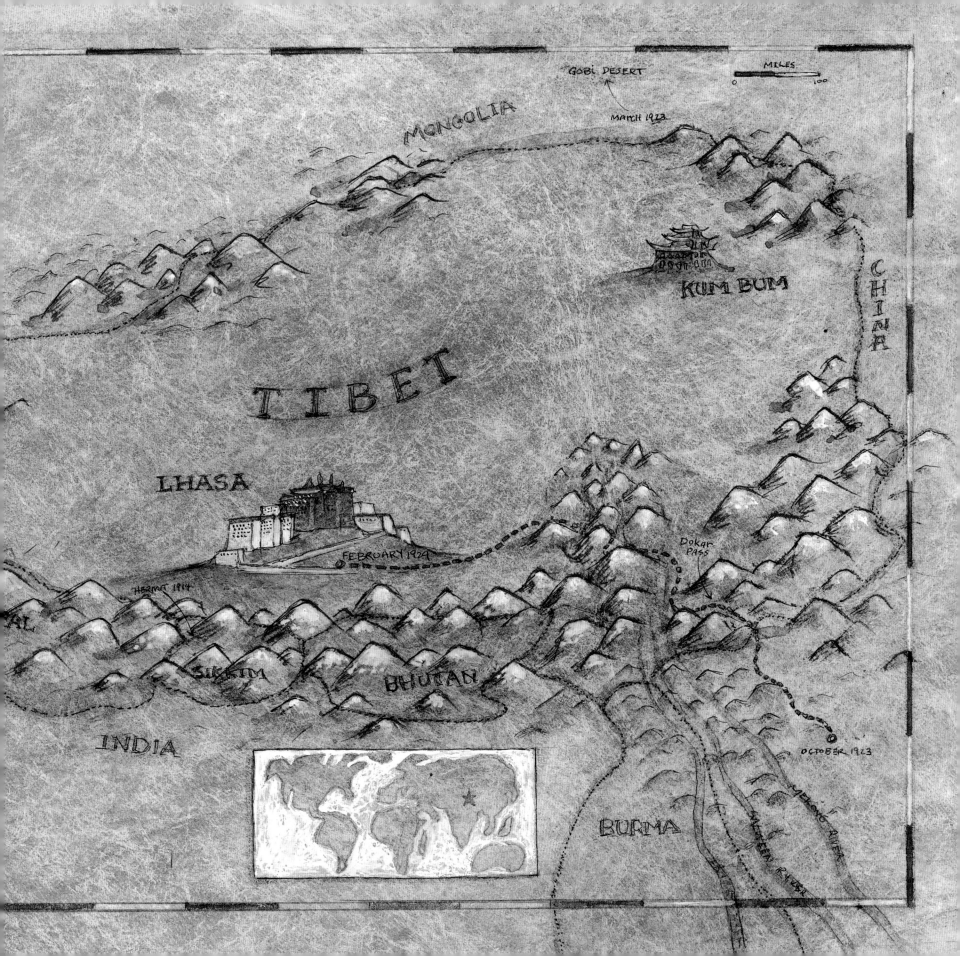

Alexandra studies music, too. After she has grown, her singing talent finds her work in far-flung places—India, Greece, and North Africa.

After more than seven years of performing with opera troupes, Alexandra settles in Tunis, North Africa, and marries Philip Neel in 1904. But thoughts of wild hills and impassable glaciers still pull on her. They finally wrest her away in 1911, when forty-three-year-old Alexandra David-Neel becomes a pilgrim to those childhood desires and sets out for Asia.

She does not see Philip for fourteen years.

Paris and Beyond

In 1873, five-year-old Alexandra David lives comfortably in Paris, France. There is a governess to watch her and toys to amuse her. But young Alexandra prefers the company of travel and adventure books and a globe instead of a doll.

"I craved to go beyond the garden gate, to follow the road that passed it by, and set out for the unknown," she later recalled. "I dreamed of wild hills, immense deserted steppes, and impassable landscapes of glaciers!"

But young Alexandra's extraordinary dreams don't fit her ordinary world; she explores faraway places only in books and museums. Still, it is through books and museums that Alexandra discovers Buddhism, an ancient Asian religion. Her enthusiasm for Buddhism and the culture of Asia entwines with her spirit.

Dokar Pass

"May all things be happy!" exclaims Alexandra upon finally reaching Dokar Pass, a 15,000-foot-high slot through the towering Himalaya Mountains. It is one of her favorite wishes.

Only the wind answers her; she and her traveling companion, Yongden, are alone. They start downhill as night falls, a devilish wind swirling thick snow around them. The narrow path disappears beneath a gloomy froth of darkness and storm. They halt, plant their staffs, cling together, and wait for the blizzard to end. It will blow through the night.

Alexandra has dreamed of this for fifty years.

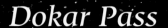

Tibet

In search of old Buddhist books and manu-
scripts, Alexandra treks through India to Tibet.
It is a remote land ruled by the Dalai Lama, in
whom lives the spirit of Buddha, the founder
of the religion.

Giant mountains ring Tibet like ramparts.
Winds race undisturbed across immense
tablelands thousands of feet high—the highest
region on earth, it is called the Roof of the
World. Buddhist monasteries dot the landscape. There, monks called lamas practice their
faith. Towns are few, and many Tibetans tramp
the landscape, as unhindered as the wind.
They are accompanied by their yaks, which
provide food, clothing, and transportation.
Even the yaks' droppings are used; they are
burned as fuel after they have dried.

Tibet captivates Alexandra. But Tibetans
distrust outsiders and forbid them to wander
their land freely. Alexandra must be content
with studying Buddhism on Tibet's rim.

She becomes the student of a scholarly hermit and spends nearly a year perched atop a mountain, learning to speak Tibetan.

A high-ranking lama grants Alexandra permission to visit the great monastery at Kum Bum in northern Tibet. She treks 2,000 miles to reach it and spends three years there translating ancient books. To Alexandra, Kum Bum is something out of a dream, a Shangri-la.

During this time, a fifteen-year-old boy called Yongden becomes her servant. Her interests are his; Yongden will become Alexandra's partner in adventure and most faithful friend.

To Lhasa

By 1923, Alexandra and Yongden, now a grown man, have journeyed thousands of miles over the Gobi Desert and across China, and have made forays into Tibet. She has become a great scholar of Buddhism and Tibet, but Alexandra still longs to move about Tibet as freely as a Tibetan and is frustrated by the barriers that stop her from visiting Lhasa, the seat of Buddhist Tibet. Only a few European men have been there and no non-Asian woman. It is called the Forbidden City.

Alexandra adopts a daring idea: She will go to Lhasa.

"Many travelers had been stopped on their way to Lhasa, and had accepted failure. I would not. . . . I would reach Lhasa and show what the will of a woman could achieve!" she said.

Her plan is simple: She will masquerade as Yongden's poor mother. They will claim to be beggars on a religious pilgrimage. So that her complexion resembles a Tibetan's, Alexandra darkens her face with cocoa powder and charcoal. She completes the costume by blackening her hair with Chinese ink and lengthening it by adding yak hair. The pair carries a pot, a knife, chopsticks, and two bowls and spoons. Beneath her robe, Alexandra hides money, a compass, and a revolver.

Into what mad adventure am I about to throw myself? Alexandra wonders as she and Yongden slip into Tibet.

They struggle through high mountain gates, including Dokar Pass, and march over carpets of snow that seem to unfurl endlessly before them.

"Behind extended the waste I had crossed," she recalled. "In front of me was a precipitous fall of the mountain. The moon rose [and] the impassive landscape . . . seemed to awaken under the blue light . . . sparks glittered to and fro, and faint sounds were wafted by the wind."

They hike beyond the mountain passes into river valleys. Alexandra falls through the ice of a frozen river and plunges into hip-deep water. Her thick dress stiffens and freezes.

Blocked by a rocky gorge, the travelers must cross by cable.

"A Tibetan girl and I were bound with rough straps, and tied together to a wooden hook that would glide us on the leather cable," Alexandra remembered. "The ferrymen began their work. Each jerk . . . at the long towing rope caused us to dance in the air a most unpleasant kind of jig."

Alexandra and Yongden tramp for miles through silent forests. Clearings reveal "shining snow-clad mountains, towering high in the blue sky, frozen torrents and glittering waterfalls hanging like gigantic . . . curtains from the rugged rocks."

A wolf trots by them with the "busy but calm gait of a serious gentleman going to attend some affair of importance."

Once, the pair shares a room with a poor farm couple and their cow, calves, and baby pigs.

Their marches are fueled by simple meals—many times only Tibetan-style tea made with butter and salt, or a thin soup of barley flour and bacon that reminds Alexandra of dishwater.

"My father's dogs would never have eaten such a thing," she joked.

Alexandra and Yongden camp in abandoned shacks and caves, and beneath trees.

They beg for hospitality at isolated farms and hamlets. At times, Alexandra fends off attacking guard dogs with her staff. Other times, she and Yongden are offered rest in courtyards and upon the flat roofs of Tibetan homes.

Countless tiny paper flags decorate the lower branches of a huge tree; earlier travelers left these goodwill prayers for those who follow.

They trek for days, for weeks. Their lives hang on the whim of the wild land and the generosity of the Tibetans.

Then, in the light of a rising sun, they see the Potala, the majestic palace
of the Dalai Lama.

The Potala, sitting like a fortress on a high hill with its many golden roofs
gleaming in the blue sky. The Potala, in Lhasa.

After four months of mad adventure, Alexandra has reached her goal.
Every hour of danger and fatigue she and Yongden have endured is repaid.
It is a pilgrim's victory.

"We have won," she tells Yongden.

And, perhaps, the wind from Dokar Pass murmurs a faint echo, "May all things be happy!"

Author's Note

Alexandra David was born outside Paris in 1868. She had an irresistible wanderlust and was fascinated by railway lines, "fancying the many lands toward which they led." She begged for gifts of travel books and maps, and, while a schoolgirl, distressed her parents by running away on journeys covering hundreds of miles. And it was as a schoolgirl that she discovered Buddhism and embarked on its lifelong study.

Alexandra had a talent for singing, and she enjoyed modest success performing opera in the Middle and Far East. In 1904 she retired from the stage, settled in Tunis, North Africa, and married Philip Neel. But her craving for travel and her curiosity about Buddhism were undeniable. With Philip's agreement, she set out alone for India in 1911. Alexandra was forty-three.

Over the next fourteen years, she befriended a mountain prince; interviewed Tibet's spiritual leader, the Dalai Lama; lived as a hermit in the Himalaya Mountains; traveled to Japan, Korea, and the Gobi Desert; and studied ancient Buddhist texts at the Kum Bum Monastery. She met Yongden, and together they trekked thousands of miles, including a grueling journey to Lhasa, the Tibetan capital, in February 1924. The visit was the first by a Western woman.

Alexandra David-Neel returned to France with Yongden, whom she adopted. But Asia tugged at her, and, now nearly seventy years old, she traveled back to Tibet in 1937. She stayed until the fighting of the Second World War drove her away.

World-renowned adventuress and Buddhist scholar Alexandra David-Neel died in 1969. She was 101. Shortly before her death, she renewed her passport. She dreamed of wild hills till the end.

Bibliography

Annaud, Jean-Jacques. *The Seven Years in Tibet: Screenplay and Story Behind the Film.* New York: Newmarket Press, 1997.

Baldizzone, Tiziana and Gianni. *Tibet: Journey to the Forbidden City.* New York: Stewart, Tabori & Chang, 1996.

David-Neel, Alexandra. *Magic and Mystery in Tibet.* New Hyde Park, N.Y.: University Books, 1956.

———. *My Journey to Lhasa.* Boston: Beacon Press, 1993.

Farrer-Hall, Gill. *The World of the Dalai Lama.* Wheaton, Ill.: Theosophical Publishing, 1998.

Foster, Barbara and Michael. *The Secret Lives of Alexandra David-Neel.* Woodstock, N.Y.: Overlook Press, 1998.

Harrer, Heinrich. *Seven Years in Tibet.* New York: Putnam, 1996.

Hedin, Sven. *My Life As an Explorer.* Garden City, N.Y.: Garden City Publishing, 1925.

Middleton, Ruth. *Alexandra David-Neel: Portrait of an Adventurer.* Boston: Shambhala, 1989.

Miller, Luree. *On Top of the World.* New York: Paddington Press, 1976.

Normanton, Simon. *Tibet: The Lost Civilization.* New York: Viking, 1989.